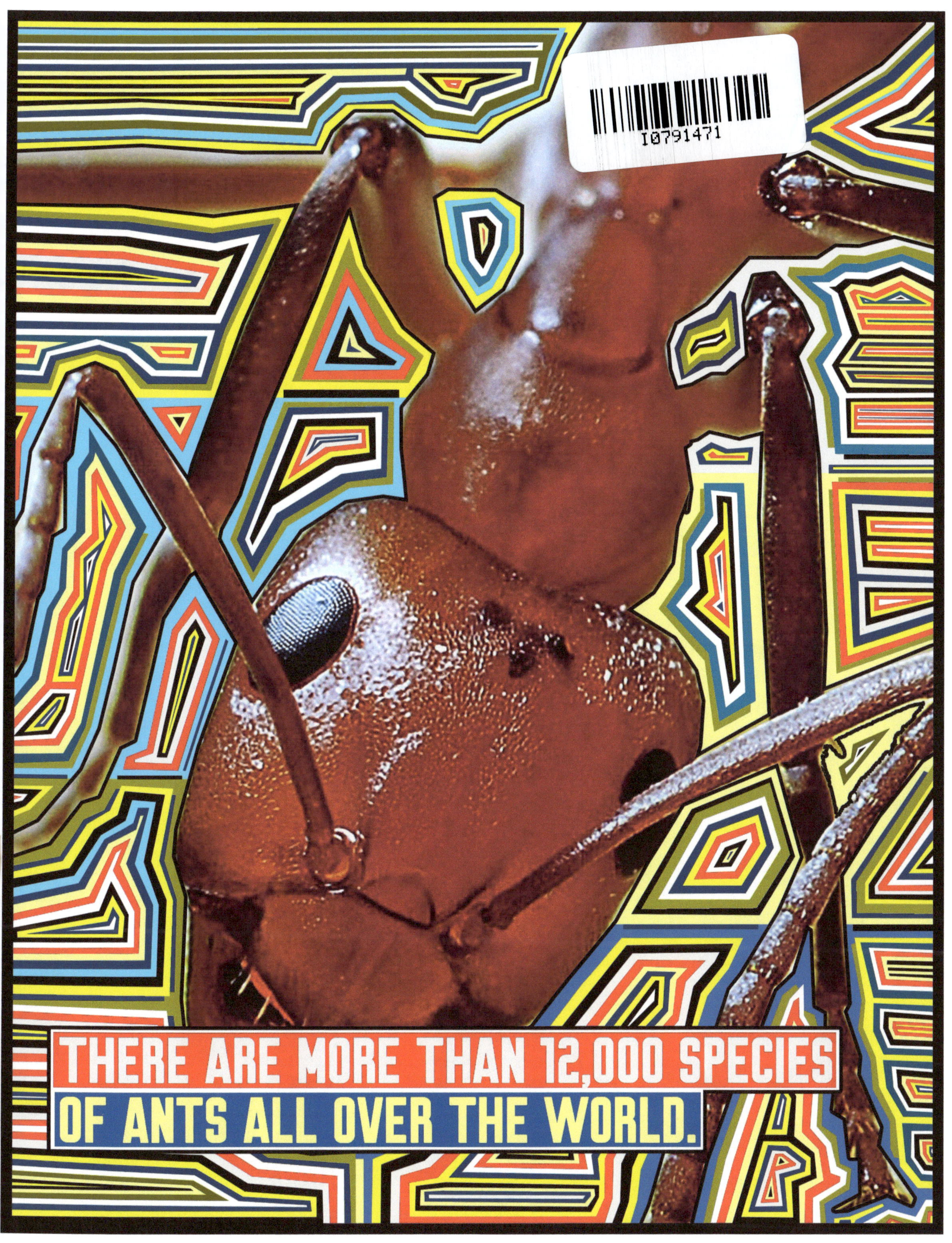
THERE ARE MORE THAN 12,000 SPECIES
OF ANTS ALL OVER THE WORLD.

AN ANT CAN LIFT 20 TIMES ITS OWN BODY WEIGHT.

INSTEAD OF A SINGLE QUEEN TENDED BY WORKERS, A YELLOW ANT SUPERCOLONY CONTAINS DOZENS OF QUEENS.
YELLOW ANT

HARVESTER ANTS ARE LARGER THAN MOST ANTS. QUEEN HARVESTER ANTS ARE AT LEAST A HALF-INCH LONG WHILE WORKERS ARE ABOUT HALF THAT SIZE.
RED HARVESTER ANT

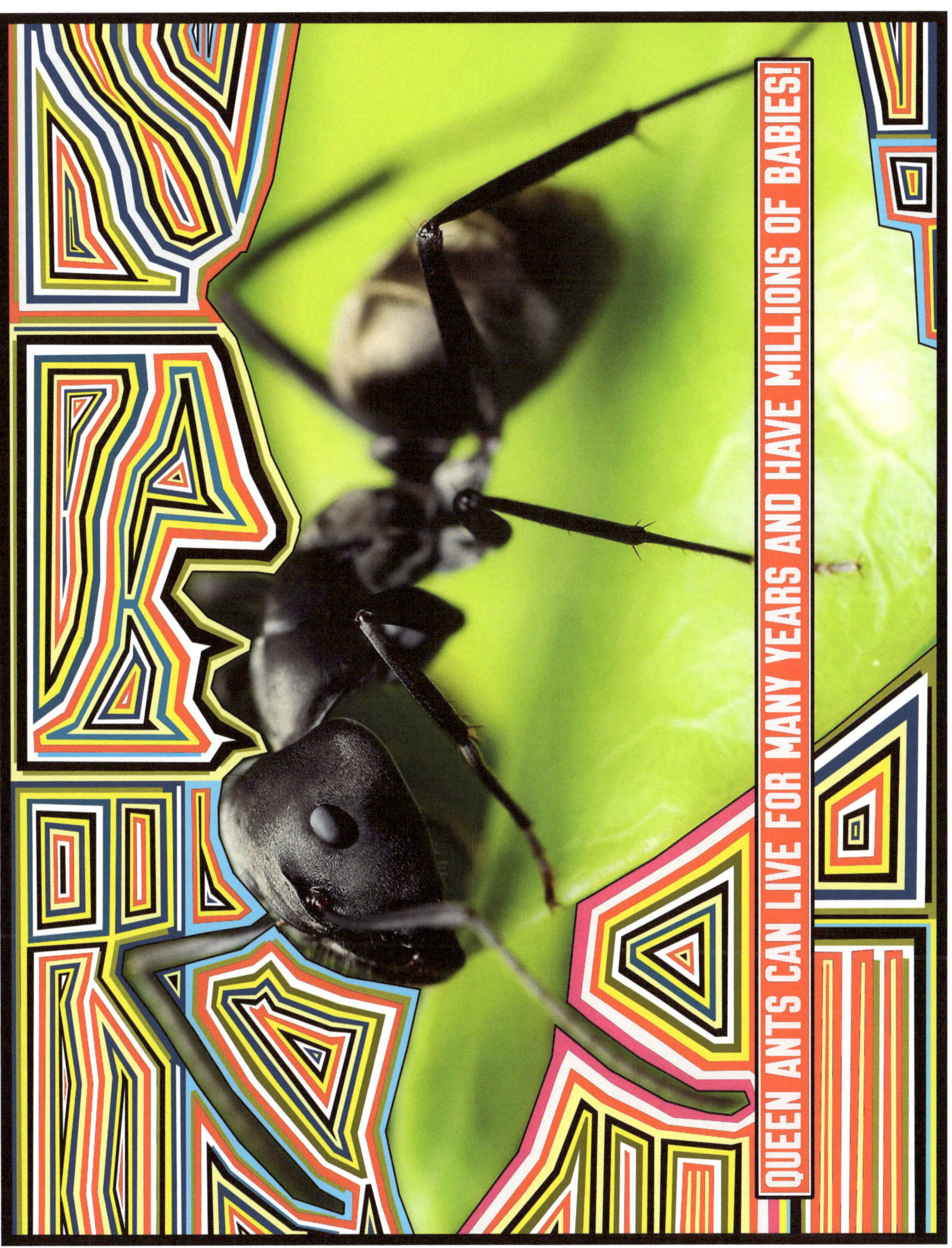

QUEEN ANTS CAN LIVE FOR MANY YEARS AND HAVE MILLIONS OF BABIES!

ANTS DON'T HAVE EARS. ANTS "HEAR" BY FEELING
VIBRATIONS IN THE GROUND THROUGH THEIR FEET.

ANTS DON'T HAVE LUNGS. OXYGEN ENTERS THROUGH TINY HOLES ALL OVER THEIR BODY AND CARBON DIOXIDE LEAVES THROUGH THE SAME HOLES.

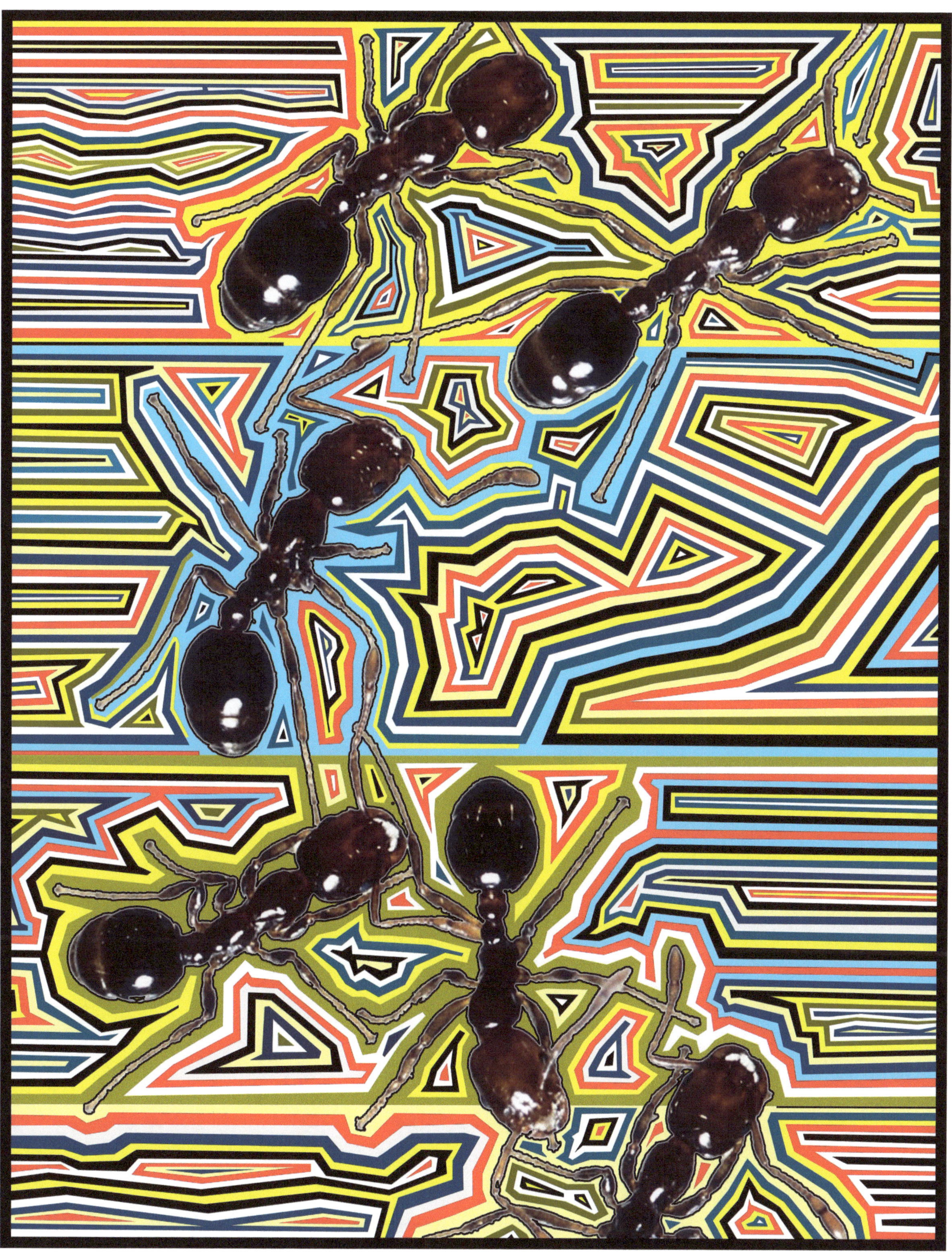

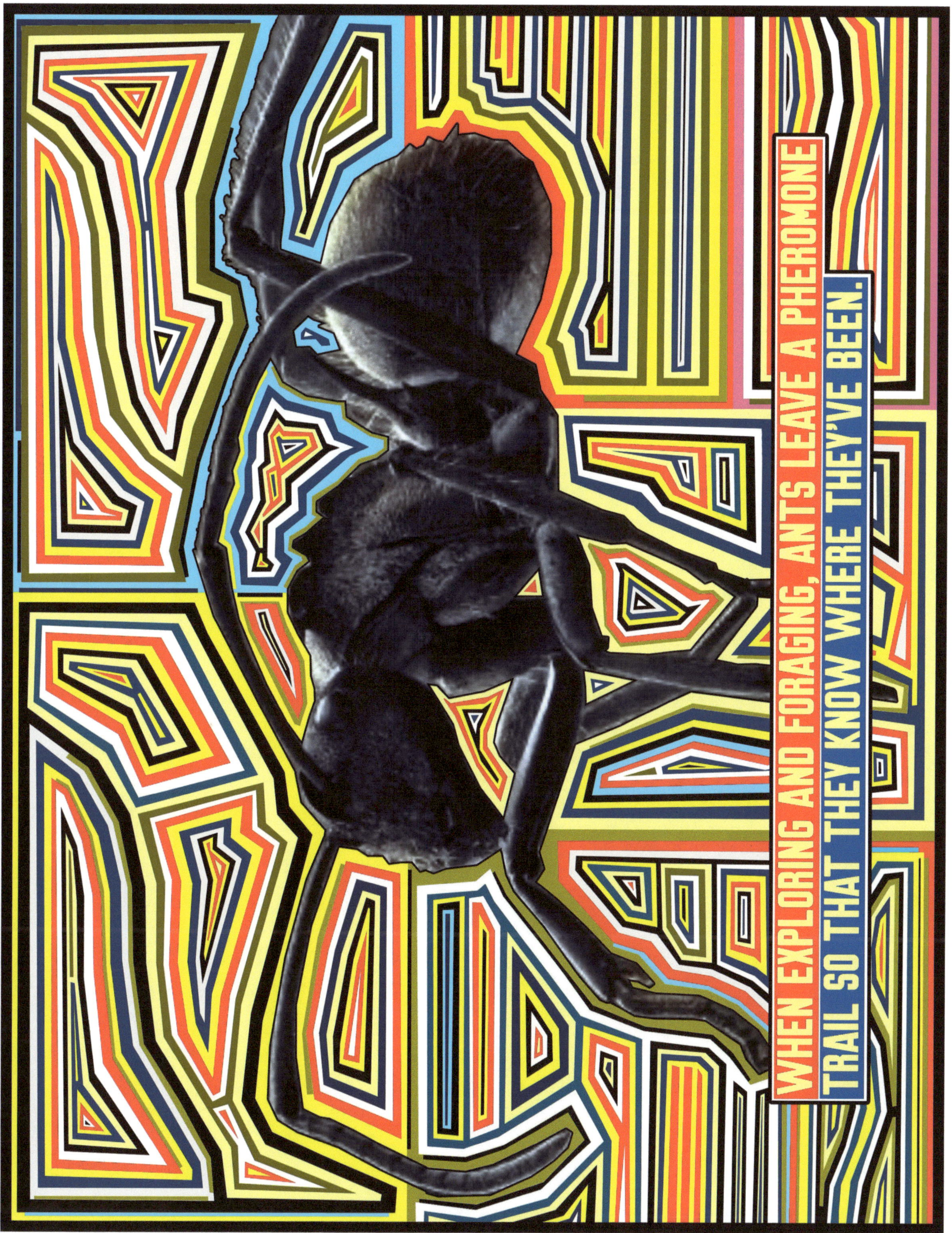
WHEN EXPLORING AND FORAGING, ANTS LEAVE A PHEROMONE TRAIL SO THAT THEY KNOW WHERE THEY'VE BEEN.

IT IS ESTIMATED THAT THERE ARE AROUND 1 MILLION ANTS FOR EVERY 1 HUMAN IN THE WORLD!

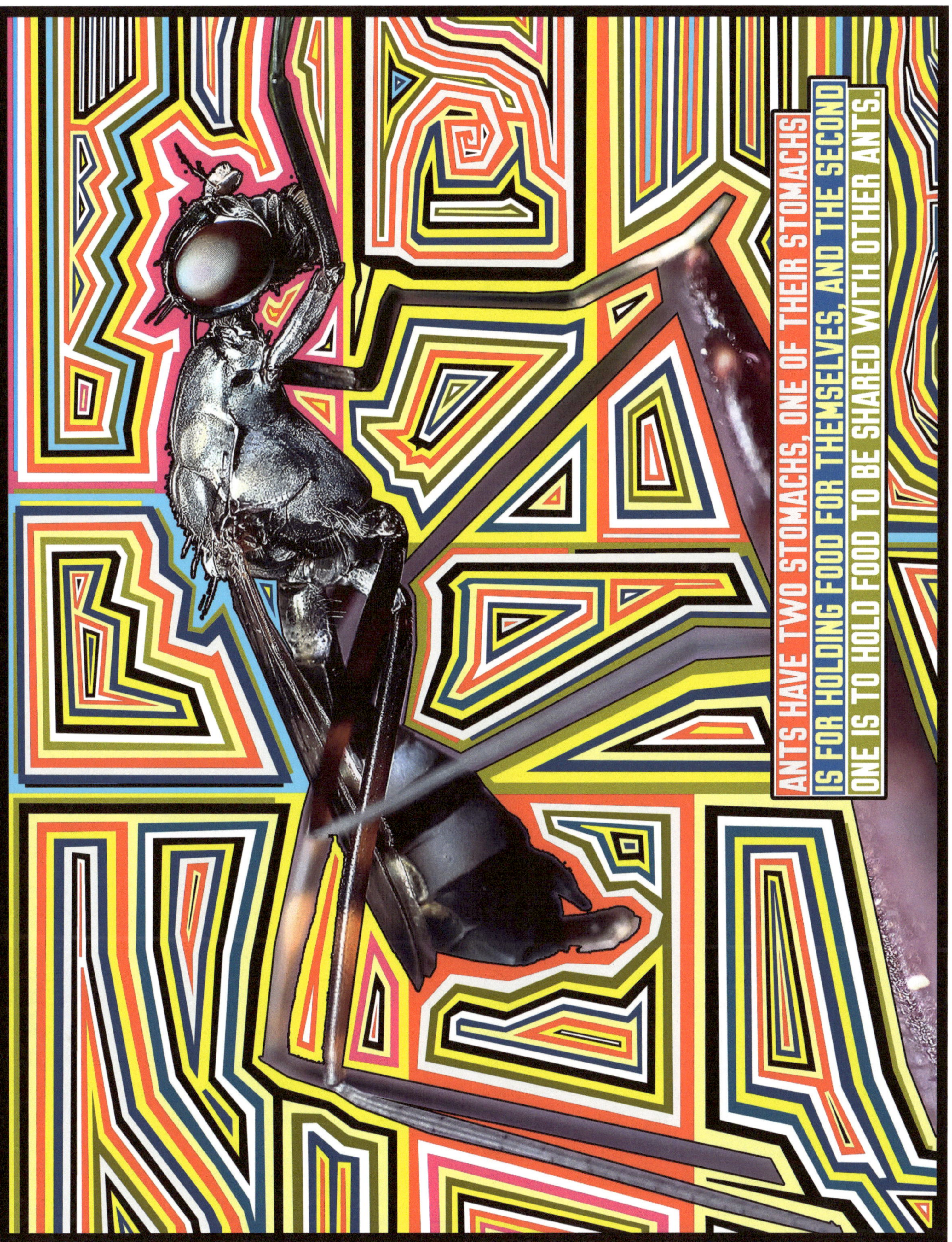

ANTS HAVE TWO STOMACHS, ONE OF THEIR STOMACHS IS FOR HOLDING FOOD FOR THEMSELVES, AND THE SECOND ONE IS TO HOLD FOOD TO BE SHARED WITH OTHER ANTS.

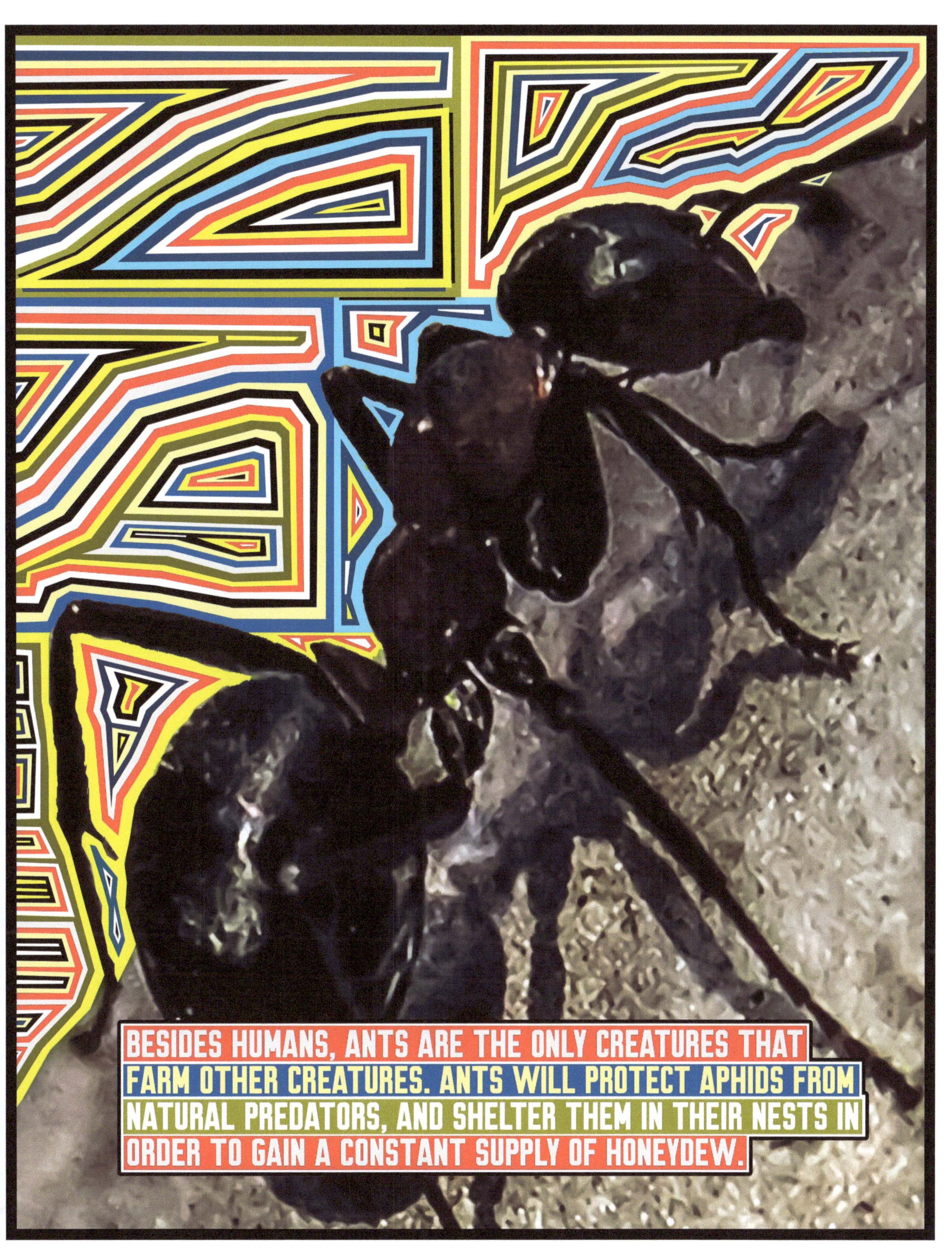
BESIDES HUMANS, ANTS ARE THE ONLY CREATURES THAT FARM OTHER CREATURES. ANTS WILL PROTECT APHIDS FROM NATURAL PREDATORS, AND SHELTER THEM IN THEIR NESTS IN ORDER TO GAIN A CONSTANT SUPPLY OF HONEYDEW.

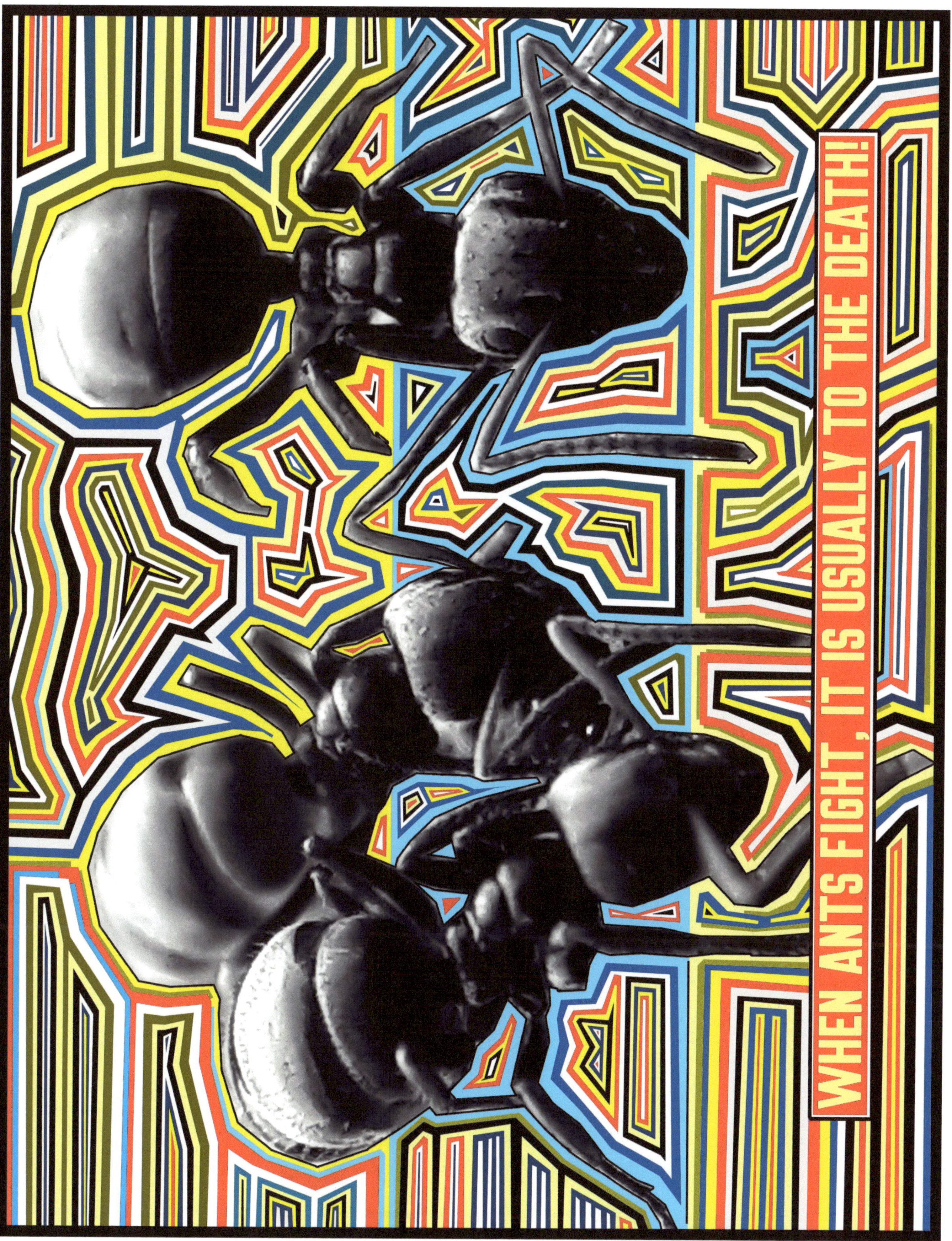
WHEN ANTS FIGHT, IT IS USUALLY TO THE DEATH!

ANTS ARE INCREDIBLE SURVIVORS. THEY HOLD THEIR BREATH UNDERWATER FOR LONG PERIODS OF TIME, AND BUILD LIFEBOATS TO SURVIVE FLOODS. SOME ANTS CAN EVEN SWIM!

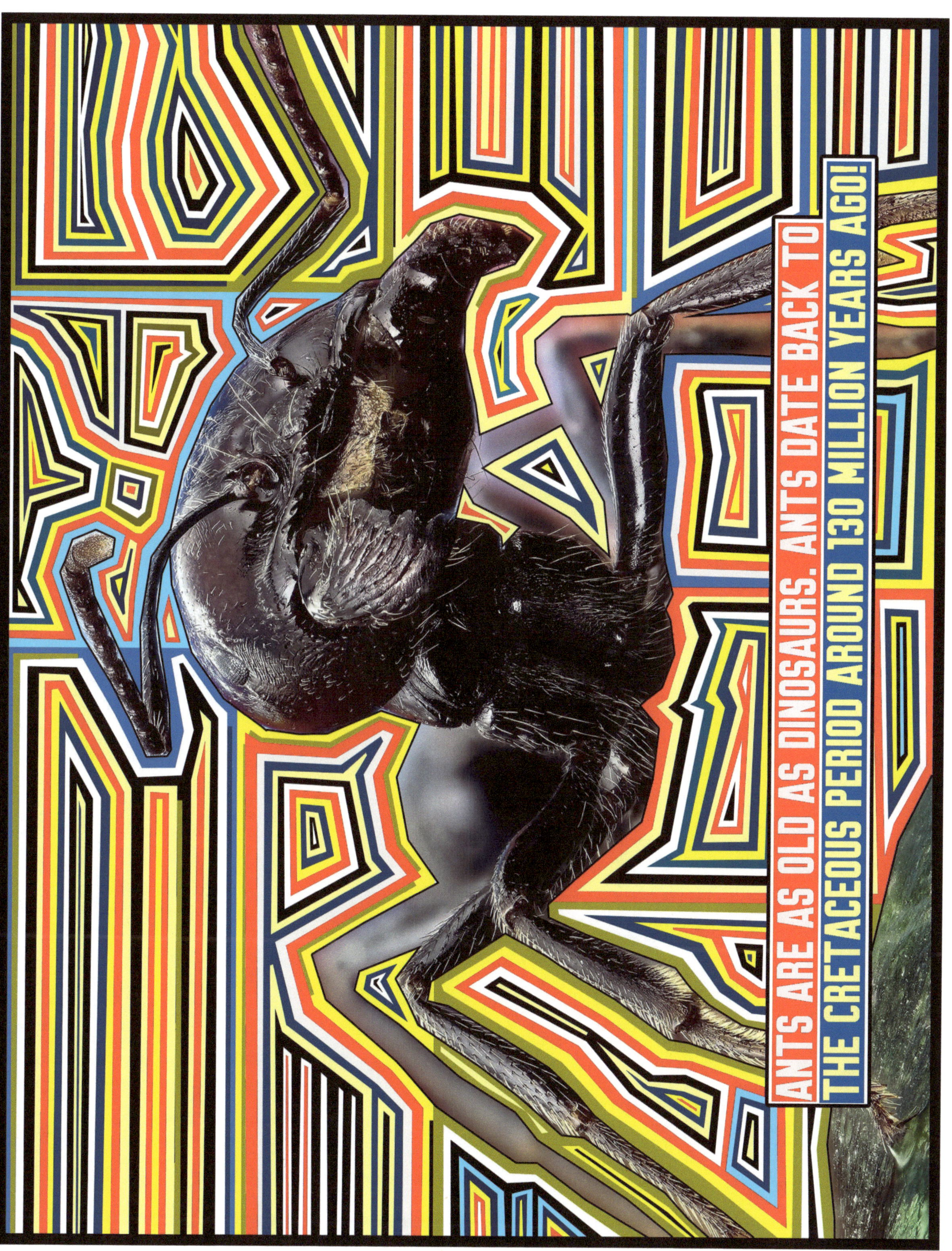
ANTS ARE AS OLD AS DINOSAURS. ANTS DATE BACK TO THE CRETACEOUS PERIOD AROUND 130 MILLION YEARS AGO!

ANTS ARE VERY SOCIAL INSECTS, AND THEY DIVIDE JOBS
AMONG DIFFERENT TYPES OF ANTS IN EACH COLONY.

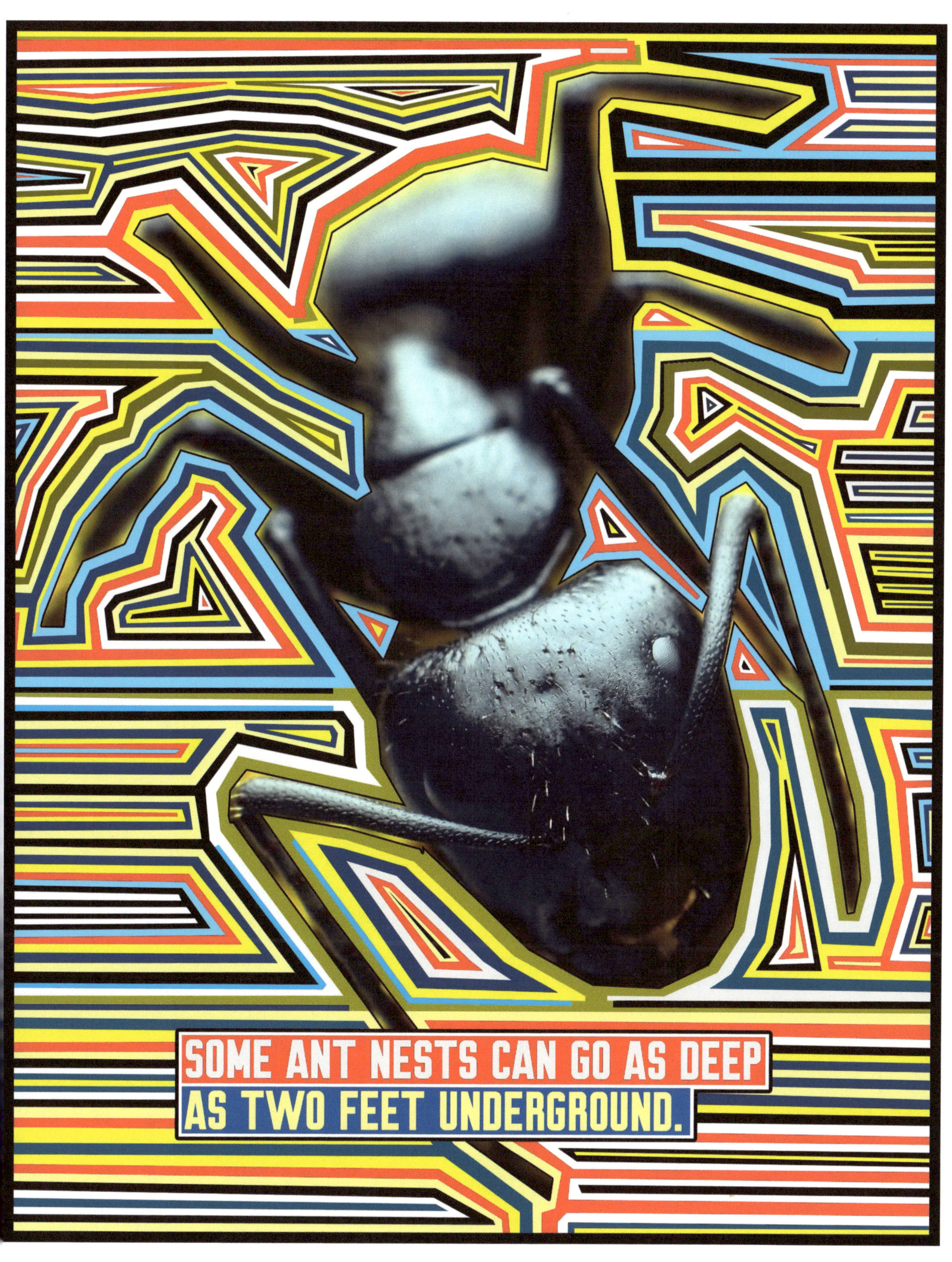

SOME ANT NESTS CAN GO AS DEEP
AS TWO FEET UNDERGROUND.

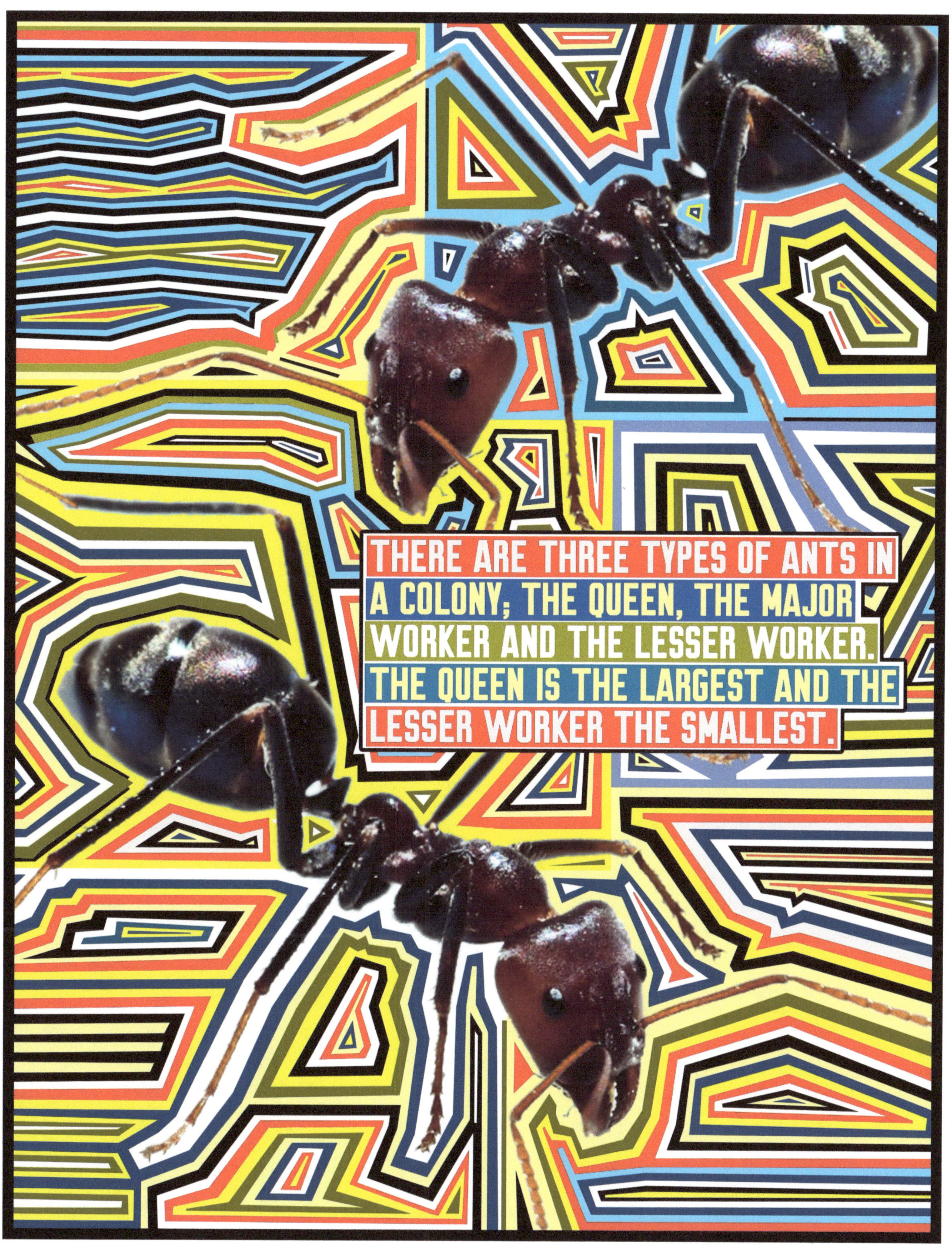
THERE ARE THREE TYPES OF ANTS IN A COLONY; THE QUEEN, THE MAJOR WORKER AND THE LESSER WORKER. THE QUEEN IS THE LARGEST AND THE LESSER WORKER THE SMALLEST.

AN ANT THE SIZE OF A HUMAN COULD
RUN AS FAST AS A RACE HORSE!

ANTS CREATE SUPERBRAINS! THEY MAY BE SMALL, BUT THEY CAN COME TOGETHER AS HUGE GROUPS AND USE THEIR INTELLECT AS A WHOLE.

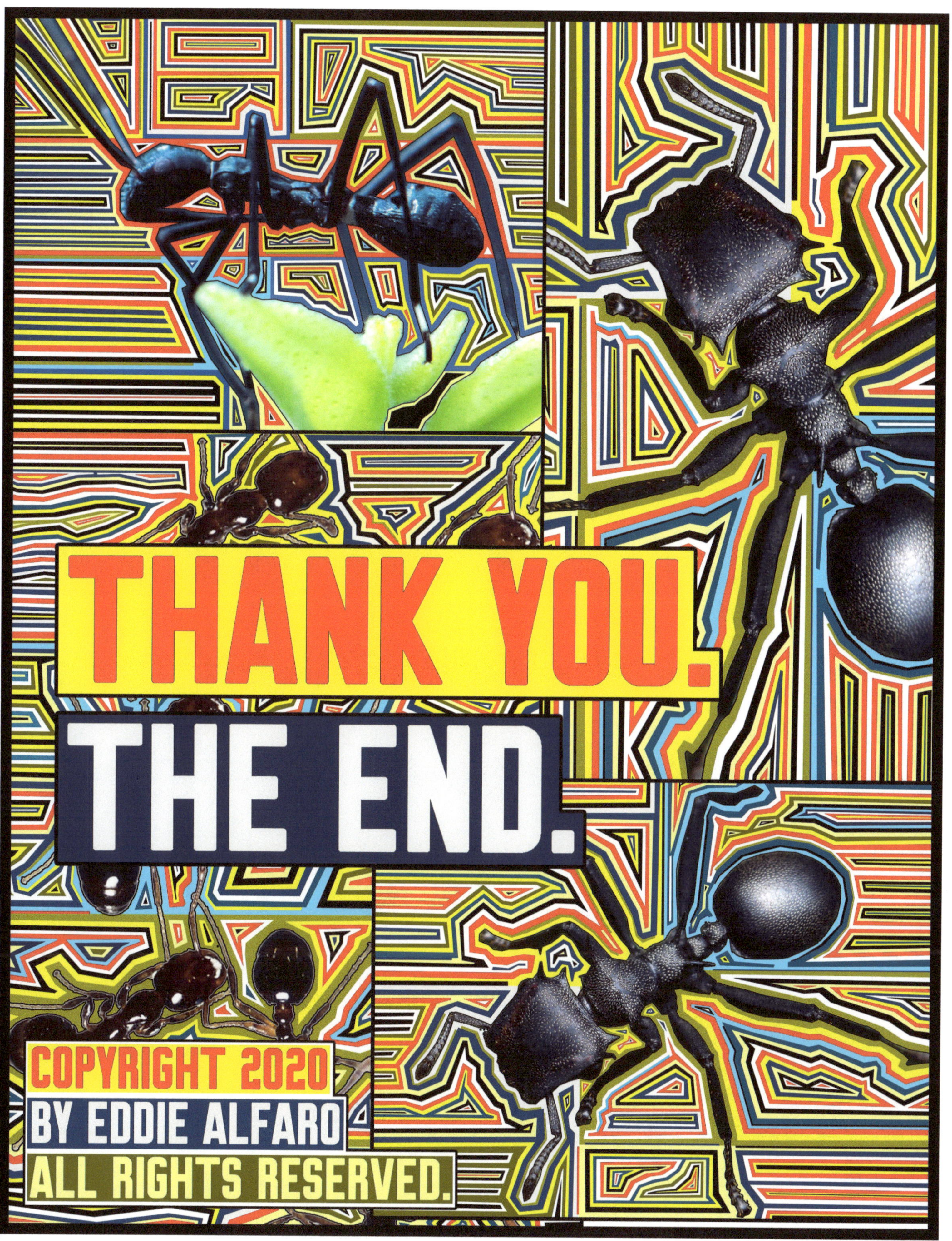
THANK YOU.
THE END.
COPYRIGHT 2020
BY EDDIE ALFARO
ALL RIGHTS RESERVED.

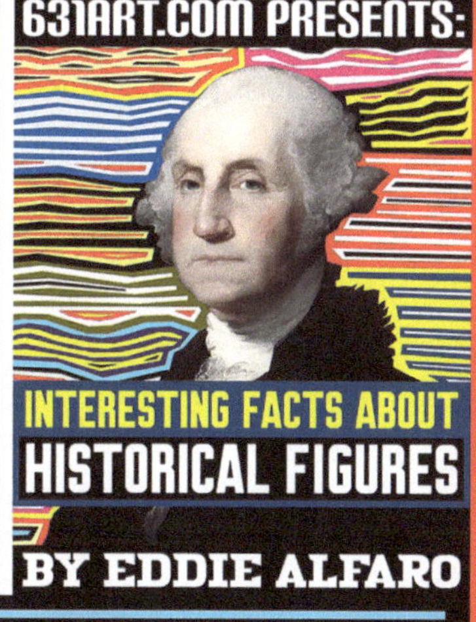

MORE BOOKS AT:

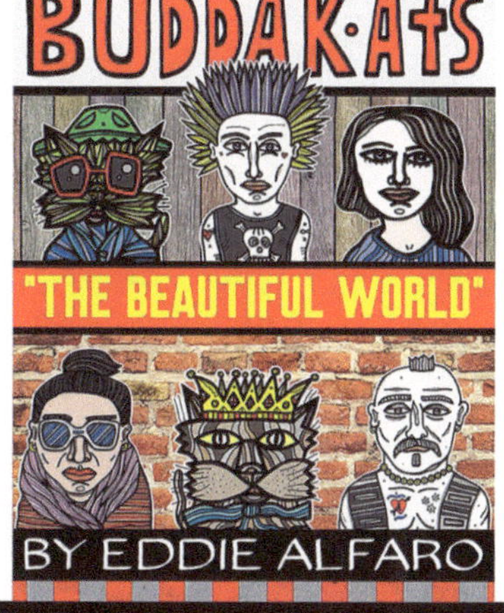

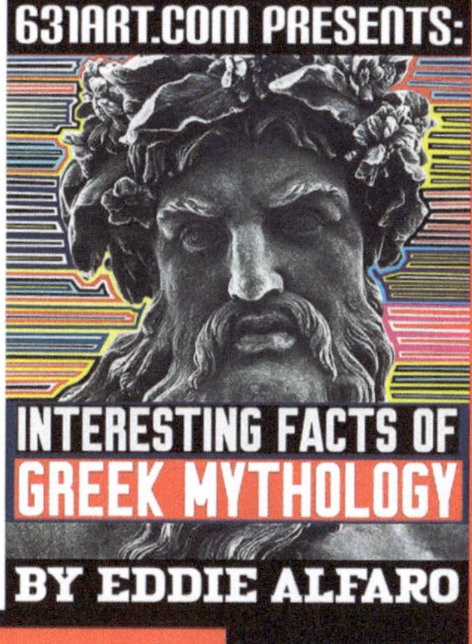

631ART.COM

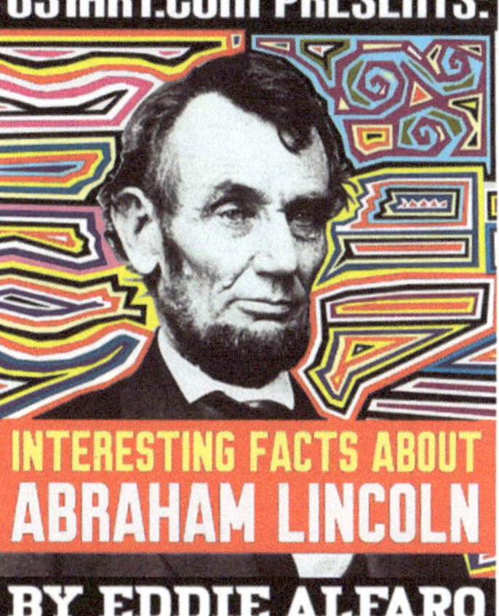

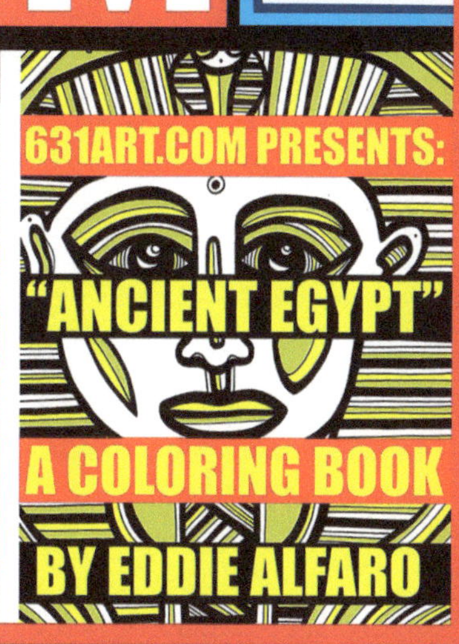